Amaya's Adventures
The Queen of Words

Dr. B

ILLUSTRATOR: ELENA ZAKHAROVA

Text copyright © 2018 S3 Publishing, Villa Shuriell Bodden
Cover imagery copyright © 2018 S3 Publishing, Villa Shuriell Bodden
Illustration copyright © 2018 S3 PublishingVilla Shuriell Bodden ,

All rights reserved. No part of this publication may be reproduced, distributed, or transmitted in any form or by any means, including photocopying, recording, or other electronic or mechanical methods, without the prior written permission of the publisher, except in the case of brief quotations embodied in critical reviews and certain other noncommercial uses permitted by copyright law. For permission requests, write to the publisher, addressed "Attention: Permissions Coordinator," at the address below

S3 Publishing LLC

2162 Spring Stuebner Rd
Ste 140 PMB 222
Spring, Tx 77389
(281)793-5913
Contact@SThreepublishing.com

Ordering Information:
Quantity sales. Special discounts are available on quantity purchases by corporations, associations, and others. For details, contact the publisher at the address above.

Printed in the United States of America
ISBN 978-1-7337300-1-3

This Book is dedicated to God

†

Not too close to here, right past over there. In between nowhere and everywhere, sparkled somewhere. Close enough to feel, far enough not to be able to touch. Shining brighter than the moon, deep in the sky, twinkled Amaya & Henry's home. Sometimes she could see it as she swung on the porch in the afternoon.

Amaya is a special child, like most of you are! Her big eyes and bright smile don't compare to the size of her heart. Every day she spends her time with Henry filling the world with love, kindness, *knowledge,* and Art. Using her shield of faith and armor, she's on a mission to fight for victory against the darkness found in unhealed hearts.

Tucked tightly in, Amaya's mom begins to read. "The *Peace-Keepers* who save the truth" she reads on and on, her voice sounds like a song.

"The truth shall prevail" she chants with excitement, all the way to the end of the chapter.

She tells Amaya the most important thing she will ever do is love herself. The second most important thing she says is to love others. She kisses Amaya's third eye, wishes her a good-night, leaving her to dreams and delights.

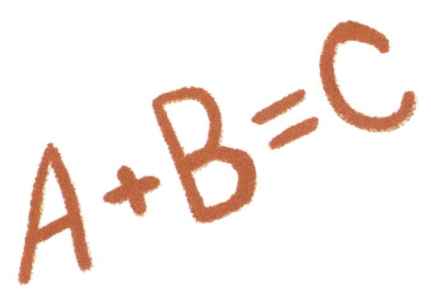

The next day at school the Rebels sat in the class delivering cruel jokes as usual. They bullied the students, especially Jalia. They bullied her because they were jealous. They hated how much she loved herself, she was *zealous.*

She loved words, and she used them well. They wished they could be like her, they wished they could spell. "Class remember the spelling bee is tomorrow" the teacher yelled into Rose's ear, who was standing next to the board eager to hear.

Henry sat outside waiting in fear, Jalia was crying…Oh dear!

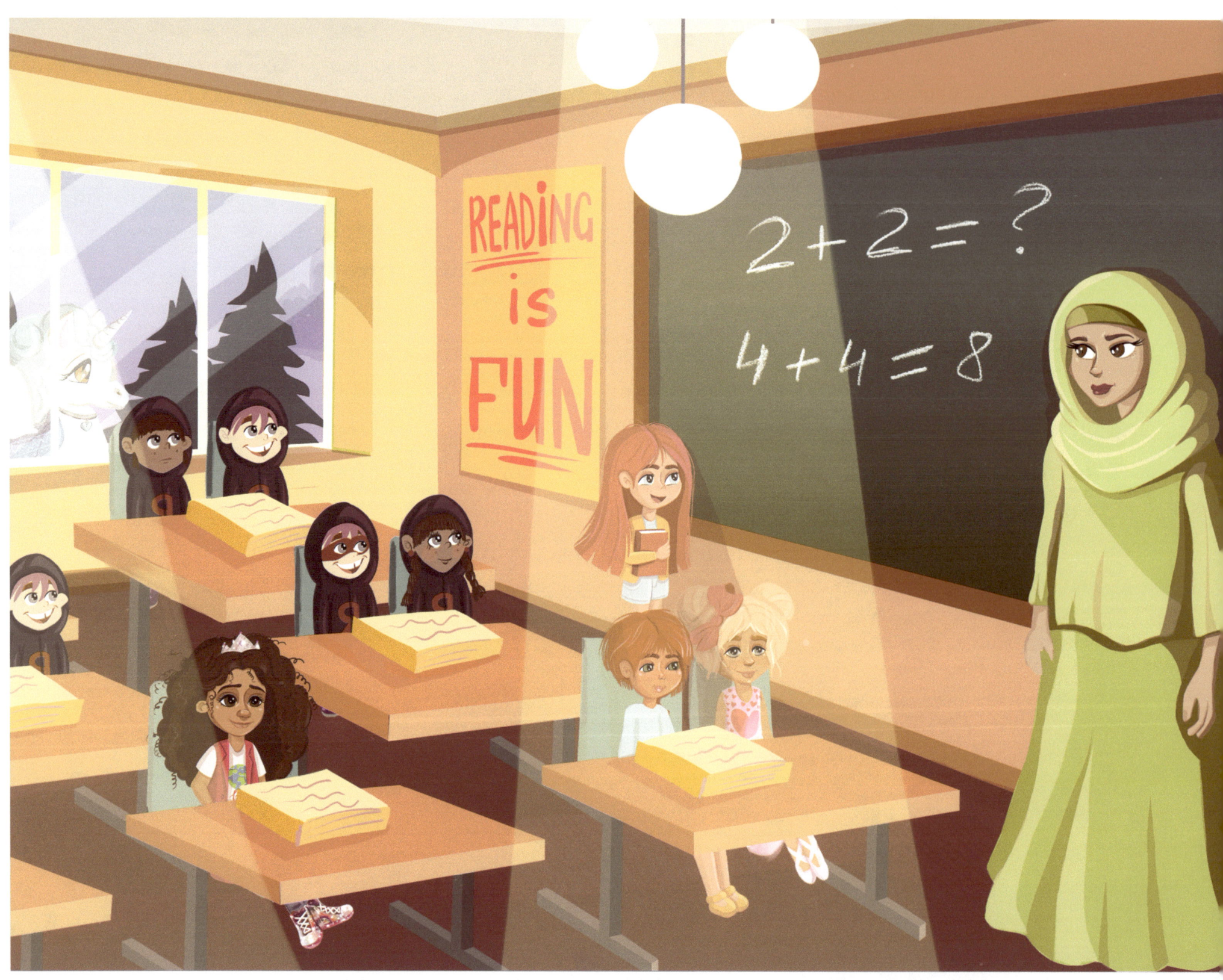

The tears flew off Jalia's face.
The pain in her heart could be seen from a mile away.
The bullying hurt so much the pain went to her head,
Jalia had a headache, "Jalia don't be upset" Amaya said with sadness for her friend.
Amaya handed Jalia Peppermint essential oil mix and told her to put it on the temples of her forehead.
"It will make your headache go away,
it works much better than *Acetaminophen* ."

It made Amaya very sad to see the Rebels hurt Jalia with their bullying. She decided to talk to her mom and brother Steve because it was so troubling. She loved and *trusted* her family, so she asked for their insight.

It's always good to ask for advice from people you *Respect* & *Trust* when you have a problem you need to make right.

Steve was older than Amaya, and he was SUPER bright.

Whenever there was a problem that Amaya and Henry couldn't solve, Steve was the first to pick it apart and make it right.

The next day started with trouble; Rose, Amaya and Henry huddled. "Apparently, the Rebels knew Jalia was really sad so they took her to the dark place" Rose mumbled. The dark Place, Henry grumbled.

The dark place is so bad the sun refuses to shine there; It's always night.

The dark place is so bad, what's wrong is always right.

Nothing good ever happens in the dark place. In the dark place people lose their hope and desire to fight.

Amaya and Rose climbed onto Henry's back and they both yelled

WORDS HAVE LIFE SHOW US WHAT'S RIGHT!
Henry activated his shield and away they went.

They could see Jalia in the distance surrounded by the Rebels' fire.

They look around for the best way to get across the *mire*.

"There" Henry said, leading them straight into the Rebels' evil plan.

Amaya grabbed her shield and led the gang across the bridge.

The Rebels attacked Henry, Rose, & Amaya with their flaming arrows.

The powerful flames cause memory loss & dreadful pain.

Amaya activates her shield of faith by yelling **"WORDS HAVE LIFE"**.

Immediately her shield of faith protected them from the burning flames.

When the Rebels realized that the shield of faith protected Amaya and her friends, they knew they had made a mistake. When the rebels saw the shield of faith, they became very afraid.

Amaya, Rose & Jalia got on Henry and ALL said

WORDS HAVE LIFE SHOW US WHAT'S RIGHT

WORDS HAVE LIFE SHOW US WHAT'S RIGHT

WORDS HAVE LIFE SHOW US WHAT'S RIGHT

"Back to the spelling bee, it's time for me to get my prize" Jalia yelled. She fought the battle of bullying and depression and won, Henry activated his spirit shield.

Arriving back at school right on time, the spelling bee was starting, and the bell chimed.

"Hello students, you all know me...I'm your English teacher, Mr. Tee" The Teacher rhymed.

"Everyone take a seat the word to spell in today's Spelling Bee is *Iridescent* Mr. Tee said happily.

"Amaya, you start," Mr. Tee said. "Your shield is *Iridescent*" please spell it for me.

" *Iridescent* "... Amaya said "E-R" then the bell chimed alerting that Amaya had lost this time.

"That is incorrect" Mr. Tee Stated, "Jalia You're next"

"Iridescent" Jalia said, " I-R-I-D-E-S-C-E-N-T, *Iridescent* ".

SPELLING

"That is correct" Mr. Tee Stated, the Winner of Prosperity Elementary school Spelling Bee Is Jalia! Jalia competed and won, claiming her crown as the Queen of words.

The Rebels lies and bullying couldn't break her down, the bullying was no match for the **WORDS OF LIFE!**

Amaya's Wisdom

Sometimes people say things that aren't nice.

You Know the *truth* ...

Believe in yourself, have faith, and do right!

Everything will be alright.

Always Remeber **WORDS HAVE LIFE!**

The words we speak to others & ourselves are really important.

SPEAK LIFE!

glossary

Acetaminophen- noun
An analgesic drug used to treat headaches, arthritis, etc. Also to reduce fever, often as an alternative to Asprin. Proprietary names include Tylenol.

Ashamed- adjective
1) Embarrassed or guilty because of one's actions, characteristics, or associations.
2) Reluctant to do something through fear of embarrassment or humiliation.

Iridescent- adjective
Showing luminous colors that seem to change when seen from different angles

Knowledge- noun
Facts, information, and skills acquired by a person through experience or education; the theoretical or practical understanding of a subject.

Mire- noun
1. A stretch of swampy or boggy ground.
2. A situation or state of difficulty, distress, or embarrassment from which it is hard to extricate oneself.

Peace-Keepers - noun
A person who tries to keep things peaceful, often by mediating conflicts or calming people down.

Prevail - Verb
1. prove more powerful than opposing forces; be victorious
2. Persuade (someone) to do something.
3. be widespread in a particular area at a particular time; be current.

Recruit- verb

1. Enlist (Someone in the armed forces)
2. Enroll (Someone) as a member or worker in an organization or as a supporter of a cause.

Respect - noun

A feeling of deep admiration for someone or something elicited by their abilities, qualities, or achievements.

Trust- noun

A firm belief in the reliability, truth, ability, or strength of someone or something.

Wage - verb

gerund or present participle: waging

carry on (a war or campaign)

Zealous- adjective

Having or showing Zeal

Zeal- noun

Great energy or enthusiasm in pursuit of a cause or an objective.

www.ingramcontent.com/pod-product-compliance
Lightning Source LLC
LaVergne TN
LVHW070408080526
838200LV00089B/364